This Land Is Our Land

by Johanna Biviano

PEARSON
Scott Foresman

Editorial Offices: Glenview, Illinois • Parsippany, New Jersey • New York, New York
Sales Offices: Needham, Massachusetts • Duluth, Georgia • Glenview, Illinois
Coppell, Texas • Ontario, California • Mesa, Arizona

Every effort has been made to secure permission and provide appropriate credit for photographic material. The publisher deeply regrets any omission and pledges to correct errors called to its attention in subsequent editions.

Unless otherwise acknowledged, all photographs are the property of Scott Foresman, a division of Pearson Education.

Photo locators denoted as follows: Top (T), Center (C), Bottom (B), Left (L), Right (R), Background (Bkgd)

Opener: Getty Images; 1 Corbis; 4 Creatas; 5 Getty Images; 6 Getty Images; 8 Digital Vision; 9 Corbis, Peter Arnold; 10 Corbis/Richard T. Nowitz, Corbis/Dave G. Houser, Stock Imagery; 11 Photo Researchers; 12 Getty Images; 13 Corbis, Getty Images; 14 Brand X Pictures, Getty Images; 15 Digital Stock, Getty Images

ISBN: 0-328-13424-4

Copyright © Pearson Education, Inc.

All Rights Reserved. Printed in the United States of America. This publication is protected by Copyright, and permission should be obtained from the publisher prior to any prohibited reproduction, storage in a retrieval system, or transmission in any form by any means, electronic, mechanical, photocopying, recording, or likewise. For information regarding permission(s), write to: Permissions Department, Scott Foresman, 1900 East Lake Avenue, Glenview, Illinois 60025.

7 8 9 10 V0G1 14 13 12 11 10 09 08

Our National Parks

America's national parks have some of the most **impressive** plants, animals, and land in nature. Suppose you are flying in a plane over these parks. Look out the window. You can see great forests, crystal rivers, flocks of birds, and herds of animals. The National Park Service was established to **preserve** this **wilderness.**

Wapati elks lie in the tall grass in Yellowstone National Park.

George Catlin, a famous artist, traveled through America in 1832. He saw great valleys and rivers. He saw buffalo herds roaming the plains. He learned about Native American life and about all the different people he met.

George Catlin worried that people coming to settle the wild lands would use it all up. He wondered how to preserve the land and the **species,** or kinds of plants and animals, on it. He hoped that people would want to protect nature.

A herd of bison grazing in the Theodore Roosevelt National Park in North Dakota

The government felt the same as George Catlin did. It wanted to make parks out of the natural wonders in America. Lawmakers decided to create a park where the Yellowstone River flowed, through parts of what we now call Montana, Wyoming, and Idaho. In 1872 Yellowstone became the first national park.

Yellowstone National Park

Historical Sites

The United States also wanted to preserve places that are important in our history. Some sites of prehistoric ruins became parks around 1900. Mesa Verde National Park in Colorado is filled with the ruins of cliff dwellings, or homes, of the ancient Pueblo people.

Cliff dwellings of Mesa Verde in Colorado

Some parks, such as the Grand Canyon in Arizona, were meant to be used for scientific learning. Scientists and other visitors can study the natural wonders of these parks.

In the eastern United States, there were not many national parks. Then the National Park Service created monuments at famous historical places. These national monuments preserve birthplaces of presidents, and battlefields and cemeteries from American wars.

National Parks

- **1872** — Yellowstone National Park (Montana, Wyoming, and Idaho)
- **1890** — Yosemite Valley National Park (California)
- **1908** — Grand Canyon National Monument (Arizona)
- **1916** — Abraham Lincoln Birthplace National Historic Site (Kentucky)
- **1936** — Colonial National Historical Park (Virginia)
- **1980** — Women's Rights National Historical Park (New York)

Yosemite Valley National Park in California

Landscapes and Wildlife

Mount McKinley is in Denali National Park, in Alaska. Mount McKinley stands 20,320 feet above sea level. It is the tallest mountain in North America.

Six million acres of land make up Denali National Park. Many different kinds of plants and animals live on its mountain **slopes.** The plants in Denali have to be tough. Most of the ground under the top layer of soil stays frozen.

Mount McKinley in Alaska

Grizzly bear

The animals in Denali have to be strong too. Only a small number of Denali's birds can stay through the harsh, long winters. Most of Denali's birds migrate south for the winter. They then return for the short summer season. They depend on Denali's lakes, rivers, streams, and ponds. **Glaciers** from ten thousand years ago made these bodies of water.

Wildlife in Denali National Park

Caribou

Another Historical Park

The Colonial National Historical Park in Virginia shows us how America looked to the first English settlers. Like Denali National Park, this park is full of impressive animals. Some of these animals are endangered. There are also acres of protected land.

Jamestown's "Old Towne" is located in the Colonial National Historical Park. Old Towne preserves the site of the first English settlement at Jamestown, founded in 1607.

You can visit the re-creation of the original Jamestown settlement.

In Old Towne, guides wear clothes like those of the first settlers. Visitors can learn about the life of Pocahontas, a famous Powhatan woman. Pocahontas helped settlers and Native Americans communicate. Visitors can also see a statue of Captain John Smith, who led the settlers in building the Jamestown Settlement. You can relive history at the Colonial National Historical Park.

Guides dress in colonial costume at Old Towne.

Preserving Wildlife

What does it mean to create a national park? When the United States chose the land for the first parks, there were no fences, no roads, no bathrooms, and no guides! Who would take care of the parks and make them easy to visit?

Most national parks have park rangers to answer questions visitors might have.

The U.S. Army was in charge in the 1890s. They made roads and buildings. They guarded the parks from hunters and loggers. They allowed people to visit the parks to learn about the wildlife. In 1916 the National Park Service was formed to run the parks. Roads and buildings in the parks were improved in the 1930s, and new parks were made.

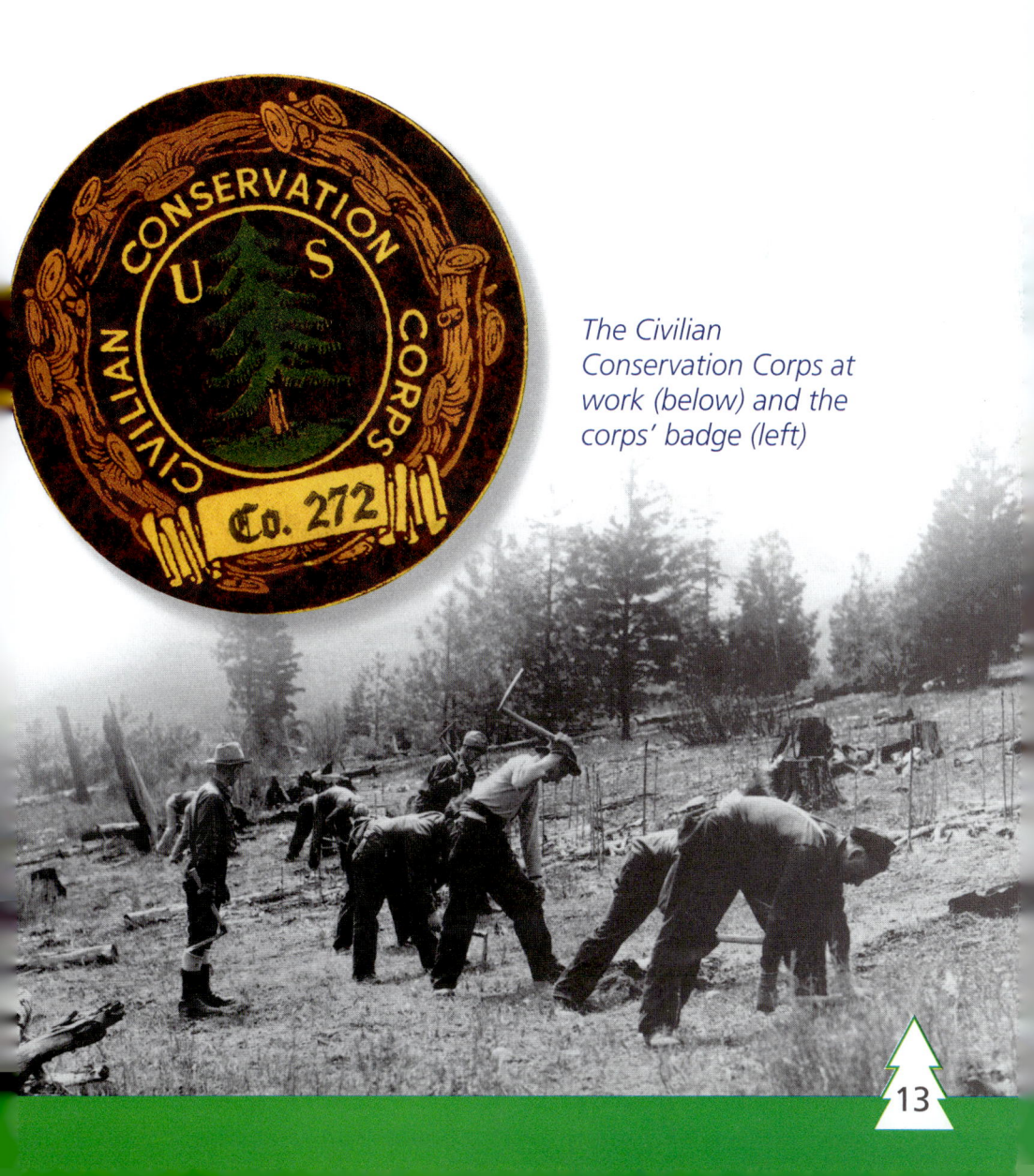

The Civilian Conservation Corps at work (below) and the corps' badge (left)

As soon as the first national park was created, people began to argue about how to use the parks. Should we let **naturalists** study the animals and plants? Should we use the rivers to water the farms nearby? Should we dig for oil? Should builders use the wood from the forests?

It is important to protect our natural wildlife.

Ibis

All of these questions now have answers. In national parks we preserve nature. We do not cut down the wood for lumber. We do not use the water for farming. All of the animals that live in the parks are kept safe from hunters. We protect the historical sites and the natural wonders of the wilderness, just as George Catlin hoped that we would!

Pika

Wolf

Glossary

glaciers *n.* great masses of ice moving very slowly down a mountain, along a valley, or over a land area.

impressive *adj.* able to have a strong effect on the mind or feelings; able to influence deeply.

naturalists *n.* people who make a study of living things.

preserve *v.* to keep from harm or change; keep safe; protect.

slopes *n.* lines, surfaces, land, etc., that go up or down at an angle.

species *n.* a set of related living things that all have certain characteristics.

wilderness *n.* a wild uncultivated region with few or no people living in it.